Black September: The History and Legacy of the Conflict Between the Palestinians and Jordan in 1970
By Charles River Editors

A picture of smoke rising near Amman during the fighting

About Charles River Editors

Charles River Editors is a boutique digital publishing company, specializing in bringing history back to life with educational and engaging books on a wide range of topics. Keep up to date with our new and free offerings with this 5 second sign up on our weekly mailing list, and visit Our Kindle Author Page to see other recently published Kindle titles.

We make these books for you and always want to know our readers' opinions, so we encourage you to leave reviews and look forward to publishing new and exciting titles each week.

Introduction

A picture of a Palestinian refugee camp near Amman, Jordan

Black September

"So long as the Arabs fight tribe against tribe, so long they will be a little people." – Lawrence of Arabia

"We had thousands of incidents of breaking the law, of attacking people. It was a very unruly state of affairs in the country and I continued to try. I went to Egypt, I called in the Arabs to help in any way they could – particularly as some of them were sponsoring some of these movements in one form or another – but without much success, and towards the end I felt I was losing control. In the last six months leading up to the crisis the army began to rebel. I had to spend most of my time running to those units that had left their positions and were going to the capital, or to some other part of Jordan, to sort out people who were attacking their families or attacking their soldiers on leave. I think that the gamble was probably the army would fracture along Palestinian-Jordanian lines. That never happened, thank God." – King Hussein of Jordan

In May 2011, President Barack Obama gave speeches about the Middle East that discussed the Israeli-Palestinian conflict, using terms like "final status issues," "1967 lines with mutually agreed swaps," and "demographic realities." Obama's speeches were strongly denounced by both the Palestinians and the Israelis, while political commentators across the world debated what Obama's speeches actually meant.

Welcome to the Middle East conflict, a conflict that is technically 63 years old and counting but has its roots in over 2,000 years of history. With so much time and history, the peace process has become laden with unique, politically sensitive concepts like the right of return, contiguous borders, secure borders, demilitarized zones, and security requirements, with players like the Quartet, Palestinian Authority, Fatah, Hamas, the Arab League and Israel. Over time, it has become exceedingly difficult for even sophisticated political pundits and followers to keep track of it all.

On May 14, 1948, the British Mandate officially expired. That same day, the Jewish National Council issued the Declaration of the Establishment of the State of Israel. About 10 minutes later, President Truman officially recognized the State of Israel, and the Soviet Union also quickly recognized Israel. However, the Palestinians and the Arab League did not recognize the new state, and the very next day, armies from Egypt, Syria, Lebanon and Iraq invaded the former British Mandate to squelch Israel, while Saudi Arabia assisted the Arab armies. Jordan would also get involved in the war, fighting the Israelis around Jerusalem. Initially, the Arab armies numbered over 20,000 soldiers, but the Zionist militia groups like the Lehi, Irgun and Haganah made it possible for Israel to quickly assemble the Israel Defense Forces, still known today simply as the IDF. By the end of 1948, the Israelis had over 60,000 soldiers and the Arab armies numbered over 50,000.

In early 1949, Israel began signing armistices with Egypt, Jordan, and Syria, which left Israel in control of nearly 75% of the lands that were to be partitioned into the two states under the 1947 plan. Jordan now occupied Judea and Samaria, which later became known as the West Bank due to its position on the western bank of the Jordan River. Jordan also occupied three quarters of Jerusalem, with the Israelis controlling only about a quarter in the western part of the city. To the west, Egypt occupied the Gaza Strip. The new armistice lines became known as the "Green Line," and the conflict has continued to involve those lines and the issues that were contested in a war now nearly 70 years old.

In 1964, the Arab League met in Cairo and formed the Palestine Liberation Organization (PLO), which intended to "liberate" Palestine and drive the Jews into the sea. At the time, Egypt and Jordan occupied the Gaza Strip and West Bank respectively, which the PLO had no interest in contesting. The PLO Charter stated, "This Organization does not exercise any territorial sovereignty over the West Bank in the Hashemite Kingdom of Jordan, or on the Gaza Strip." Although the PLO became the most famous Palestinian organization, it actually consisted of several independently operating groups. The most noteworthy of them was Fatah, which had been founded in 1956 and had been conducting attacks on Israeli targets since its inception. Among the members of Fatah was Yasser Arafat, who would soon become the most visible face of the PLO. Other main groups within the PLO included Popular Front for the Liberation of Palestine and the Popular Democratic Front for the Liberation of Palestine, which essentially were militant groups.

In early June 1967, the Israelis captured Jordanian intelligence that indicated an invasion was imminent. On June 5, the Israelis launched a preemptive attack that knocked out the air forces of its Arab neighbors. Over the next six days, the Israelis overwhelmed the Egyptians in the west, destroying thousands of tanks and capturing the Gaza Strip and the entire Sinai Peninsula. At the same time, Israel drove the Jordanians out of Jerusalem and the West Bank, and it captured the Golan Heights from Syria near the border of Lebanon.

With realities changing on the ground, Palestinian resistance changed tactics and locations, and the tension caused by Palestinian attacks originating from Jordan would eventually lead to the expulsion of the PLO from Jordan. Before then, however, the notorious Black September would launch one of the most famous terrorist attacks of the 20th century at the Olympics in Munich in 1972, and that would touch off some of the Israeli Mossad's most legendary operations as the Israelis sought to track down those responsible for the attack.

Black September: The History and Legacy of the Conflict Between the Palestinians and Jordan in 1970 looks at the fighting and its effects on the Middle East. Along with pictures and a bibliography, you will learn about Black September like never before.

Black September: The History and Legacy of the Conflict Between the Palestinians and Jordan in 1970

About Charles River Editors

Introduction

   Jordan and Palestine

   Palestinian Nationalism

   Black September

   The Aftermath

   Online Resources

   Further Reading

Free Books by Charles River Editors

Discounted Books by Charles River Editors

Jordan and Palestine

The Kingdom of Jordan came into being as a consequence of the difficult circumstances associated with the British withdrawal from Palestine. The history of the Middle East, so multilayered and complicated as to defy any possibility of brief explanation, nonetheless acquired its modern form largely in the wake of World War I. Prior to this, the Arab world, from the eastern Mediterranean to the Caspian Sea, and from the Balkans to North Africa, and south along both shores of the Red Sea, lay under the control of the Ottoman Empire, governed from the Turkish capital of Constantinople.

The central portion of the Ottoman Empire, comprising much of what would today be Egypt, the Levant, western Iraq and most of Turkey, was ruled directly from Constantinople under the usual terms of imperial government. This implies a territorial governor answering directly to the Sublime Porte, or the central authority of the empire, often governing a bureaucracy comprising career civil servants on deployment to the various colonies. Looser systems of government tended to apply to regions on the fringe of the empire, which offered varying degrees of autonomy to local leadership under the broad suzerainty of the central, Ottoman government. Often, a successful rule in this regard was achieved by a simple divide and rule policy, playing mutually antagonistic tribes against one another. This was the same basic method of imperial government and control affected by all of the major empires of the time, although the Ottoman Empire was considerably more ancient than the British, French, Russian or German Empires.

The Ottoman Empire, which was fundamentally a religious, Muslim empire, began to slip into decline as secular nationalism gradually began to take root in Europe, and as the rise of nation-states began to supersede the old European monarchies. The 1908 "Young Turk Revolution" altered the political structure of the empire, ending the absolute rule of the Sultan, in this case, Sultan Abdul Hamid II, and introducing the Second Constitutional Era, and the revival of the Ottoman Parliament. Multi-party democracy began to take shape at the center of the empire, which weakened it, a process that was compounded by the subsequent and rapid secession of the territories of Greece, Bulgaria, Bosnia and Herzegovina. Rebellions, needless to say, began popping up here and there, which eroded the cohesion of the outer empire.

The British, in the meanwhile, then the first among equals of European imperial powers, took effective control of Egypt, followed by Malta, which catalyzed European interest in cherry-picking portions of the Ottoman Empire to augment their own. During this period the territories of Algeria and Tunisia passed into the French sphere of influence, Libya into the Italian sphere of influence.

The eastern Mediterranean, however, comprising the Levant and the Hejaz region of the Arabian Peninsular, remained firmly fixed in the Ottoman Empire, and in 1900, a railroad was constructed from Damascus to Medina, bringing the Hejaz and the holy sites of Islam under firmer Ottoman control.

The situation on the Arabian Peninsular was a complicated one, and the traditional bonds of Ottoman control, never particularly strong, began to disintegrate as the leaders of the various Arab kingdoms began to sense religious discrimination at the hands of the new, democratic Turks. Traditionally the Ottomans had not run their empire as the Roman Empire, for example, or to a lesser extent, the British and French. They did not attempt to culturally or constitutionally integrate the various tribes and peoples that fell under their control, allowing instead a wide scope of religious and cultural separation. As a consequence, nationalism found fertile ground throughout the empire, with little incentive on the part of the ruling elites to remain loyal to the center. Identities tended to be local, and thus, when push came to shove, loyalty to local leadership tended to supersede identity with the empire.

As the preamble to World War I played out in Europe, the Germans sought the alliance of the Ottoman Turks, and eventually, when guns began firing along the Western Front, the Turks were indeed among the Central Powers. The Middle East, and in particular the Suez Canal zone and the east and west shores of the Red Sea, suddenly became regions of great strategic significance to both sides, and most of these fell under the control of the Ottomans. Add to this the oil interests in Mesopotamia, and the potential for major European power plays throughout the Arab region was huge.

In 1916, seizing the opportunity to fulfill an age-old ambition, then Sharif of Mecca, Hussein ibn Ali al-Hashimi, launched a rebellion against Ottoman rule. This rebellion, known as the Arab Revolt of 1916, although ostensibly pertaining to the entire Arabian Peninsular, really only affected the region of the Hejaz and those parts of the Arabian Peninsular bordering the Red Sea and the Levant. The British, established in Egypt and astride the Suez Canal, recognized immediately the strategic advantage in supporting an Arab uprising in the Hejaz region, and this they did. The rebellion was led primarily by Hussein Ibn Ali's three older sons, Faisal, Abdulla, and Ali. The British appointed a permanent liaison to the Arabs in the form of Colonel T.E. Lawrence, the fabled Lawrence of Arabia, who organized and largely led an Arab guerrilla force against the local Turkish garrison.

T.E. Lawrence

At this time, the Arabs pictured a united, pan-Arab state with its capital at Damascus. From this, one can surmise that this Arab nation was pictured by the Arabs themselves as including the entire Arabian Peninsula and the Levant, with further interests in North Africa. It was an ambitious concept, rendered practical only because the British offered a firm commitment to support the Arabs in the achievement of this enormous goal. The British, however, had absolutely no intention of permitting, let alone helping to facilitate, the formation of any such Arab state. Allied territorial objectives ranked far higher among British priorities than Arab, and in fact, the British and the French had already decided the future fate of almost the entire region. On May 16, 1916, an Anglo-French agreement, styled the Sykes-Picot Agreement, was ratified, wherein both powers agreed to carve up the old Ottoman, Levantine and Arab possessions among themselves as soon as an inevitable Allied victory in the war could be achieved.

Colonel Lawrence, as political liaison to the Arabs, could not have been entirely unaware of British intentions in this regard, but it appears that he either did not fully appreciate them or felt them to be negotiable, and as such he remained the diplomatic face of British assurances to the Arabs. However, when he marched into Damascus at the head of an Arab army, accompanied by

Faisal, the leader of the revolt, he was met by British forces under General Allenby, who informed both men that the territory was to be mandated to French control. Apart from the shock that this represented to Lawrence himself, it came as a profound disappointment to the Arabs, the first of many similar disappointments that would follow as the political fate of the Middle East was played out on a European global chessboard.

After the war, the collapse of the Ottoman and German empires released from imperial control numerous minor territories, and in part, the League of Nations, the first international organization and a precursor to the United Nations, came into being as a means of providing temporary governing mandates to a number of these. Some were the German territories of Africa, which were granted either to the French, Belgians or the British, as well as the various territories ceded by the Ottoman Empire. These governing mandates were temporary in nature and intended to fill a vacuum of power in the immediate aftermath of the war. The British were granted a governing mandate over Iraq, as well as the area that now comprises Israel, the West Bank, the Gaza Strip and Jordan, while the French assumed control of the mandated territory of Syria, which included Lebanon.

These acquisitions temporarily expanded British and French imperial reach, but Britain was now confronted with the difficult practicalities of reconciling the conflicting nationalistic ideals between Arabs and Jews over the same territory, while also bearing in mind both had been promised British aid in achieving their national goals. In short order, the decision was taken to divide the British mandated territory of the Levant into two, so the area east of the River Jordan became the Emirate of Transjordan, ruled by Faysal's brother Abdallah, and the territory lying to the west of the Jordan River became the British mandate of Palestine. This marked the first time in modern history that Palestine became an official and united political entity.

Naturally, these turns of events angered the wider Arab population and leadership, and a sense of betrayal was inevitable. The mandate system and the assumption of control by France and Britain was seen by Arabs as a naked betrayal, thwarting their aspirations for self-rule and opening the way for accelerated Jewish immigration. Indeed, as Jewish immigration did accelerate, violence to some degree became inevitable.

The first open clashes between Arabs and Jews began to manifest in 1920 and 1921. The basis of these clashes was centered on land, and the large-scale land purchases funded by the Jewish National Fund. These, again, concerned land held under feudal systems by absentee Arab landowners, upon which poor Arabs had lived or had access to for generations. The resettlement of Jews under more formal legal arrangements, if not directly supported by the British, were at least upheld by the British, and they generated significant tension within a region already undergoing massive change.

Land matters, however, were just part of the problem. In 1928, Muslims and Jews in Jerusalem, administered then as an international zone for its religious significance to all three of the major monotheistic religions, began to clash over their respective communal religious rights and access to the Western Wall, or the Wailing Wall. The Western Wall, which is the last surviving remnant of the Second Jewish Temple, is the holiest site in Jewish religious tradition. Above the wall is a plaza known as the Temple Mount, which is the theoretical location of the two ancient Israelite temples. However, a few hundred feet to the north lies the al-Aqsa Mosque and the Dome of the Rock, among the holiest sites in Islam. This is believed to mark the spot from which the Prophet Muhammad ascended to heaven on a winged horse, al-Buraq, which he tethered to the Western Wall, and which, in Islamic tradition, bears the horse's name.

A picture of the Western Wall and the al-Aqsa Mosque

These violent clashes were centered on religious tradition, and have different causes depending on who one chooses to believe. It is generally accepted, however, that they began on August 15, 1929, as members of the Betar Movement, a Revisionist Zionist youth organization, raised the Zionist flag, featuring the Star of David, over the Western Wall. One can assume that a certain amount of physical demonstration accompanied this, and the Arab response, probably no less provocative, was to demonstrate in opposition. However it started, there were subsequent attacks against Jews in Jerusalem, Hebron and Safed, with over 60 Jews killed in the initial clashes. As a result, the Jewish community of Hebron evacuated to Jerusalem, and in the week or so of communal clashes that followed, 133 Jews and 115 Arabs were killed, with many more displaced or injured on both sides.

In 1920, the British appointed Sir Herbert Samuel High Commissioner of Palestine, hoping, it was claimed, to strike a balance between the two communities. The communities, however, were by then so hopelessly polarized that not even this conspicuous, and rather belated attempt at even-handed administration could control Jewish expansion, or address the increasingly violent expressions of Arab anxiety. The riots that broke out within a year of Sir Herbert's arrival nonetheless compelled him to introduce restrictions on Jewish immigration, henceforth to be governed by the "economic absorptive capacity" of Palestine.

Sir Herbert Samuel

As the strike continued, violence increased. There were attacks on British troops and police posts, as well as on Jewish settlements, and the sabotage of roads, railways, pipelines and so on. The British introduced curfews and brought in imperial troop reinforcements, and although martial law was not introduced, emergency regulations were employed, including mass arrests, collective fines and internments.

At the same time, the Jews were not passive in response, and the primary vehicle of Jewish reprisals was the Haganah, a Jewish paramilitary organization that would subsequently form the core of the Israeli Defense Force. Some 2,800 Jews were also inducted into the police as supernumeraries, which again did not dispel a conviction on the Arab side of British favoritism towards the Jews.

Palestinian Arab resistance to British control and Zionist settlement climaxed with the Arab Revolt of 1936-1939. This marked the beginning of organized Arab nationalism in Palestine, a phenomenon that the British had been tempted to ignore in the face of more obvious and organized Zionist nationalism. It grew out of similar nationalist agitation in Egypt and Syria, which had forced both the French and the British to open treaty negotiations with each.

In April 1936, what began as minor clashes between Arabs and Jews turned rapidly into a widespread revolt. A union of Palestinian Arab political parties was formed under what was called the Arab Higher Committee, led by the Mufti of Jerusalem, Al-Hajj Amin al-Husseini, and a general strike was called in support of Arab nationalist demands for a national government.

Amin al-Husseini

Much of the basis of this revolt was Arab alarm, not only at ongoing Jewish immigration, but at apparent British complicity, and the extent to which the British seemed to be susceptible to Zionist pressure. The British had made certain clear and unambiguous pledges to the Arabs, which now appeared to have been abandoned in favor of the creation of a Jewish state, and it was obviously difficult for the British to argue against this. The British, however, were also reminded frequently of their undertaking to provide for Jews in the Mandate of Palestine.

The strike was called off in October 1936, and the British turned to the heads of neighboring Arab states to mediate while Whitehall authorized a Royal Commission, the Peel Commission, to study the causes of the "disturbances." The findings of the Peel Commission were published on July 7, 1937, and in a candid report, they concluded that the League of Nations Mandate was not working. Instead, the report proposed the partition of Palestine. The Arab Higher Committee absolutely rejected the proposition, opposing in totality the idea of any iteration of a Jewish state and calling instead for an independent Palestine with appropriate protections for all legitimate Jewish and other minority rights, and the safeguarding of reasonable British interests. They also demanded an immediate halt to Jewish immigration and land purchases, arguing again that the creation of a Jewish state and the lack of an independent Palestine was a betrayal of World War I pledges given by the British.

Restrictions imposed on Jewish immigration to Palestine remained in place throughout World War II and continued in the aftermath, even as millions of displaced Jews throughout Europe sought sanctuary from the horror of the Holocaust, the true extent of which was only then being fully appreciated. There was an obvious unwillingness on the part of many East European Jews to return to their ruined communities, and a mass movement of Jews within and out of Europe began. The British established a quota of 18,000 a year, which all but made legal immigration impossible for the hundreds of thousands of Jews trying to get into Palestine. Thousands were intercepted and interred in camps in Cyprus.

Britain, now facing the reality of decolonization and the winding down of the British Empire, rapidly lost its appetite to deal with what was an increasing intractable problem, so in February 1947, the British announced their intention to relinquish the governing mandate over the territory of Palestine. By then, the League of Nations had been superseded by the United Nations as the global governing body, and the matter was therefore submitted to the General Assembly to be resolved. The British anticipated a single-state solution and was quietly hopeful that the Arab majority population would carry the day. The United States, on the other hand, now more forceful in international affairs, pressed for a solution more favorable to the Jews.

In May 1947, a United Nations Special Committee, UNSCOP, was established to investigate and make recommendations for the future of Palestine. The Jewish Agency lobbied for Jewish representation on the committee, and also, in a sign of a more hawkish and confident Zionist mood, for the exclusion of both Britain and Arab countries. It also pressed hard for the committee to include visits to camps where Holocaust survivors were interned in Europe as part of its brief. The Arab states, on the other hand, convinced that Arab statehood in Palestine was under threat, and unwilling to acknowledge the United Nations justification over the matter, argued that the rule of Palestine should revert to its inhabitants, in accordance with the provisions of the Charter of the United Nations, or that the matter should be put before an International Court. The Arab Higher Committee, therefore, refused to cooperate with UNSCOP.

In August 1947, a majority report of the United Nations Special Committee recommended that the region be partitioned into separate Arab and Jewish states. This was followed, on November 29, 1947, by a vote of the United Nations General Assembly that ratified the plan, and put it into existence. The terms of the plan were contained in Resolution 181, and the most important result was that the land would be partitioned in such a way as to ensure that each state would have a majority of its own population. Nonetheless, inevitably, some Jewish settlements would fall within the proposed Arab state, while hundreds of thousands of Palestinian Arabs would become part of the proposed Jewish state. The area designated for the Jewish state would also be slightly larger than the Arab state, in the expectation of accelerated Jewish immigration at the moment that Jewish autonomy was achieved. Jerusalem and Bethlehem would become international zones under United Nations administration.

Each state would comprise three major sections, linked by extraterritorial crossroads, and the Arabs would also gain an enclave at Jaffa. With about 32% of the population, the Jews would be allocated 56% of the land, containing a population of roughly 499,000 Jews and 438,000 Arabs, but most of this territory comprised the Negev Desert of the south. The Arabs would get 42% of the land, with a population of 818,000 Palestinian Arabs and some 10,000 Jews.

While that partition sounds lopsided at first glance, it's important to recall, as Zionists at the time pointed out, that Transjordan, which was granted independence by the British in 1946, had comprised 75% of the entire land under British control, meaning the proposed Jewish state would end up comprising less than 15% of the entire Mandate while two Arab countries got the other 85%.

Publicly, the Zionist Jewish leadership accepted this plan, acknowledging it as "the indispensable minimum." The Arabs, on the other hand, rejected the plan entirely, regarding the whole process, including the General Assembly vote, as an international betrayal.

The Israeli declaration of independence took place on May 14, 1948, and almost immediately a combined Arab force invaded the new territory, intending to crush the concept of Israel before it could come into being. As a consequence of this war, hundreds of thousands of Palestinian Arabs were displaced, with most ending up in what were seen as a temporary refugee settlement in Jordanian, Syrian and Lebanese territory. There is also a school of thought, backed up by some credible historical research, that the Arab leaders encouraged the Palestinians to leave their homes and land on the understanding that they would return upon the annihilation of Israel, at which point Palestine would number itself among Arab nations. Either way, be it by expulsion or exodus, significant numbers of Palestinian Arabs left the war zone and became refugees.

Defying all the odds, the Israelis won a comprehensive victory, and not only was the state of Israel secured, Israeli territorial allocations were expanded upon. This had the effect of creating a permanent population of Palestinian refugees in Israel's neighboring countries, especially Lebanon and Jordan. Jordan, however, retained the territory of the West Bank as a result of the war, and it held control of East Jerusalem, which hosted a large population of Palestinian Arabs. Jordan formally annexed the West Bank on April 24, 1950, which was not a popular move anywhere except Jordan itself. The Syrians too were now in occupation of the Golan Heights, a strategic location overlooking the agricultural heartland of Israel, which was a threat the Israelis felt very uncomfortable under.

During the decisive Six Day War in 1967, Israel captured all of the West Bank, the Sinai, the Gaza Strip, and the Golan Heights. The loss of both the West Bank and East Jerusalem was critical to Jordan on many levels. Mostly it was crucial because of the historic loss of Hashemite custodianship of the al-Aqsa Mosque, the third holiest site in Islam, but also the practical loss of revenue associated with controlling the old part of the most important city for all three major religions of the world. Then there was the question of the West Bank, where a large population of Palestinian Arabs resided. Needless to say, a new wave of Palestinian refugees fled not only East Jerusalem, but the countryside of the West Bank itself, and many of these ended up in refugee camps in Jordan.

The vast increase of the Palestinian presence in Jordan altered the demographic balance between Palestinians and Jordanians to the point that the Palestinians outnumbered Jordanians and began to assert an increasing amount of political influence. As militant Palestinian groups began to organize and arm in order to confront Israel, they gradually became an independent force in the country, effectively creating a state within a state.

In addition to these developments, Jordan, at least during the early years of its existence, remained largely pro-West, while the rest of the Arab world began to lean increasingly in the direction of the Soviet Union. By 1952, when King Hussein, the third Hashemite king of Jordan, took the throne, the Palestinian presence in the country had become a definite threat, and some kind of armed equalization was inevitable.

This, then, was the background to the Jordanian Civil War of 1970-71, the event that the Palestinian groups involved referred to as Black September.

Palestinian Nationalism

"Palestine is the cement that holds the Arab world together, or it is the explosive that blows it apart." - Yasser Arafat

In April 1950, two years after Jordan occupied the West Bank in the aftermath of the 1948 Arab/Israeli War, the territory was formally annexed as a district of Jordan. West Bank Palestinians were given Jordanian citizenship, and Palestinians, who comprised two-thirds of the general population of the territory, enjoyed full political rights and commensurate representation and citizens of Jordan.

There were, however, many Palestinians who saw the act of Jordanian annexation of the West Bank as a de facto act of war. The West Bank had been allocated to the Arabs under United Nations Resolution 181, and the region was seen as part of a future Palestinian state, not as a province of Jordan. Indeed, the Jordanian leadership, and the Hashemite monarchy, many would say one and the same thing were in some Palestinian quarters seen more as the enemy than the Israelis. No Arab country recognized the annexation as a permanent arrangement, and nor, for that matter, did the United States.

Nonetheless, Jordan, including the West Bank, thereafter became the main staging area for a growing movement of Palestinian guerrilla attacks against Israeli targets across the Green Line. In the aftermath of the 1948 war, a furious propaganda campaign was waged across the ideological line of Israel and the Arab states, with the latter entirely refusing to recognize Israel and denying its right to exist. The ideological objective of the Arab world, probably the only unifying policy of the entire region, was the absolute destruction of the state of Israel. The outcome of the 1948 war was not seen in any way as final, and a renewed and united Arab military effort to achieve this all-important goal was only just a matter of time.

The Arab states were not overtly supportive of direct Palestinian action in the form of cross-border attacks and guerrilla raids mounted mainly from Jordanian territory. King Hussein was, of course, extremely anxious to ensure that the armed Palestinian movement did not gain too influential a foothold in Jordan.

Of those organizations, the largest and most influential was Fatah, or the Palestinian National Liberation Movement, founded in 1959 by Yasser Arafat. The second largest, but the more leftist and militant, was the Popular Front for the Liberation of Palestine, founded by George Habash in 1967. Others include the Palestinian Liberation Front (PLF), founded in 1961, the Democratic Front for the Liberation of Palestine (DFLP), founded in 1968, and numerous other smaller factions. Collectively, they were known as the Fedayeen, an Arabic idiom meaning Freedom Fighter.

Arafat (center)

The Palestinian Liberation Organization was established on June 2, 1964, by the Arab League, as an umbrella association. It was founded in an attempt, on the one hand, to bring order into the chaotic and undisciplined Palestinian liberation movement, but also as a means for Arab governments to exercise greater control over it. In practical terms, the PLO was a surrogate organization of Egyptian President Gamal Nasser. Nasser was the original Arab nationalist, passionately anti-Israel and supportive of every movement dedicated to the destruction of Israel. He was the most vocal and belligerent of Israel's Arab neighbors, and the most committed to a final and total military solution to the blight of Israel in the Middle East. But much as Nasser supported the PLO, the fact remained that Palestinian paramilitary action against Israel, although it might have enjoyed a certain fringe appeal and satisfied the propaganda requirements of a people robbed of their national destiny, had no practical hope of ever overthrowing the Israelis. That could be achieved by an alliance of Arab states alone, and that was Nasser's objective.

The wider appeal of the PLO to militant Palestinians, therefore, was fairly limited. The polarity of the Palestinian liberation movement remained widely separated, with individual groups organizing and acting separately from one another, and often suppressed and discouraged by the governments of the countries that hosted them.

The massive Arab defeat in the 1967 changed a lot of this. The war was such an abject, dismal military failure for the Arabs that a sense of hopelessness began to prevail about destroying Israel through military force. While it once seemed possible that the mighty armies of the Arab world would rise and crush the enemy, that confidence seemed forlorn and rather hopeless. Suddenly, the idea of limited, sustained guerrilla actions began to seem less implausible. The PLO began as a consequence to develop considerable regional popularity and approval, at least among the wider Arab population, simply because of its ongoing military efforts to "liberate" Palestine.

Israel, of course, was never militarily threatened by any of these actions, but they were at least seen by the Arabs as more effective than the massive build-ups of force and enormous mobilizations that the Israelis seemed able to outmaneuver and crush with apparent ease. These Fedayeen actions, however, despite their popular appeal, were destabilizing across the region. They presented a negative image of the movement as a whole, especially as they began to assume the characteristics of terrorism, and also because they inevitably invited Israeli reprisals. For this reason, Arab governments, in an effort to rein in the independence of the PLO and to limit the collateral damage on their nations, frequently arrested PLO activists, trying at the same time to direct the organization's activities more in the direction of diplomacy.

The PLO, however, was by its nature a loosely configured association of independent political and armed groups, each with its own leadership structure and ideological orientation. Thus, it was difficult, if not impossible, to control. In February 1969, Arafat was elected chairman of the PLO, a position that he would hold until his death in 2004. Under Arafat's control, the organization developed greater legitimacy and quickly became a power to be reckoned with on the political landscape of the Middle East.

Throughout the late 1960s, the PLO's main base of operations was Jordan. However, until its seizure by the Israelis during the war in 1967, the PLO and its associated groups tended to be focused more actively on the West Bank. When Jordan lost this territory, large numbers of Palestinian refugees crossed the Jordan River into Jordan proper, as did thousands of active PLO members and other Fedayeen.

Arafat, having escaped the West Bank ahead of Israeli forces disguised as women, moved the headquarters of his Fatah organization to a location a few miles east of the Jordan River known as Karameh, and there the movement reorganized and consolidated. From there, it began to mount fresh attacks against Israel.

All of this placed King Hussein of Jordan in a very difficult position. Attacks by various PLO factions from Jordan into Israel created a situation of ongoing border tension, and Israeli reprisals into Jordon were frequent and violent. The Israelis adopted a strategy of hitting back hard every time a Palestinian attack was staged, in order that it would be fully understood by everyone involved that no hostile action against Israel would go unpunished.

King Hussein of Jordan

On March 18, 1968, an Israeli school bus detonated a landmine in southern Israel near Eilat, killing two adults and injuring up to 27 children. Israelis were outraged, and a large-scale retaliatory action was launched three days later against the Fatah camp at Karameh. The Israelis encountered heavier resistance than they had anticipated, and the attack became a full-scale battle that lasted throughout the day. The camp was destroyed, and some 200 PLO casualties were inflicted, but the Israelis also suffered casualties, losing 30 killed. Both sides claimed victory, and while the Israelis probably won a tactical victory, the PLO undoubtedly secured a propaganda triumph. In the aftermath of Karameh, the PLO and Arafat became households names in the Middle East, and the various Arab governments began to take both a great deal more seriously.

Another point worth considering is that the PLO claim of victory, even though it might not necessarily have been true, punched a hole in the aura of invincibility that the IDF had enjoyed since 1967. This lifted the spirits of all the Arab states, particularly the Palestinians, and it encouraged recruitment to the various organizations. Volunteers from across the Arab world flocked to the ranks of the Fedayeen, and within a few weeks of the battle, there were estimated to be some 20,000 armed Palestinians and Palestinian supporters in Jordan. Arms and training were offered by Iraq and Syria, and the Gulf States, led by Kuwait, raised a significant amount of money for the PLO by levying a 5% tax on the wages of all Palestinian guest workers in the emirate.

This changed the complexion of the PLO and its constituent organizations, which now began to take on the characteristics of authentic militant administrations. They offered payments, compensation, and support for men and women injured in the line of duty, and for the families of combatants killed. PLO run clinics, hospitals, and schools began to appear in the various camps and refugee settlements. Fatah ran publishing presses and propaganda branches, proliferating its own particular message and lionizing its leadership, especially Arafat, who very quickly became an object of international interest. The December 1968 edition of *Time* Magazine, for example, featured a cover image of Yasser Arafat, complete with his signature dark glasses and keffiyeh headscarf, with a ghosted image of a Kalashnikov-wielding Fedayeen behind him. The title of the piece proclaimed Arafat as the "Fedayeen Leader."

Soon, Fatah, one of the original Palestinian militant organizations, emerged as the first among equals, and within a year of the Battle of Karameh, it claimed branches and cell in 80 countries. Trailing behind was the Popular Front for the Liberation of Palestine and smaller organizations, such as the Ba'athist orientated Syrian movement As-Sa'iqa, also known as the Vanguard for the Popular Liberation War. Thus, Fatah dominated the various forums of the PLO, and through funding channeled from Kuwait, Saudi Arabia, Libya, Algeria, and Syria, it was able to establish the institutions of an international organization far more effectively than its rival groups within the PLO.

The two principal focus points of Palestinian militant activity became Egypt and Jordan. In Egypt, the PLO enjoyed unequivocal support from the government of President Nasser, but in Jordan, the situation was a little more complicated. Egypt was never part of the direct Arab-Israeli question insofar as it was not created out of the ruins of British Palestine, as had Jordan. Palestinian militants could contrive no direct claim on the government of Egypt, and so Nasser perceived no threat from them. Jordan, on the other hand, comprised a majority population of Palestinians, and it had been carved out of land traditionally populated by Palestinian Arabs before World War I. Thus, the Hashemites, of whom King Hussein was the current head, lacked, at least in the eyes of the Palestinians, legitimacy as rulers of the territory. The dynasty had been granted rule over Jordan by the British for reasons related to World War I strategy and diplomacy. King Hussein was, therefore, seen as fundamentally pro-British, and as a consequence allied to the West, while the Arab world, in general, was tilting ever more conspicuously toward the East.

All of this placed King Hussein and the Jordanian political leadership in a very difficult position. Amman, the capital of Jordan, became the center of Palestinian militancy, while the various Palestinian refugee camps and Palestinian enclaves throughout Jordan emerged as hotbeds of agitation against the monarchy and the Jordanian government. Palestinian groups were conspicuously beginning to assert themselves as an independent authority in Jordan, even as they had competing agendas and differing standards of radicalism at their core of leadership.

Clearly, the collective Palestinian objective in this regard was to challenge Hashemite rule in Jordan, with a further objective of utilizing Jordan as the basis of a Palestinian state. The two main Palestinian refugee camps of Al-Wehdat and Al-Hussein, both within the Governorate of

Amman, began to style themselves "independent republics," each establishing an independent administrative authority under the control of PLO militants, with PLO security checkpoints, an ad hoc system of justice, PLO street patrols, and a separate, informal (and occasionally extortionate) system of taxation. In practical terms, the PLO had become something of a state within a state in Jordan.

It was inevitable, therefore, that the more militant and aggressive groups under the PLO umbrella would begin to flex their muscles against the Jordanian government.

Black September

"The truth is that Jordan is Palestine and Palestine is Jordan." – King Hussein

At this point, King Hussein found himself in something a quandary. Prior to Karameh, he had been seriously contemplating some sort of a military confrontation with Palestinian militant organizations on Jordanian soil, but in the aftermath of the battle, the popularity of the movements across the wider Arab World protected them, and any action against them would certainly have invited regional diplomatic fallout.

In November 1968, King Hussein ordered a military response against a splinter group known as Al-Nasr in response to an attack against a Jordanian police post, and the result of this was a rather weak political accord known as the Seven-Point Agreement. This, in simple terms, bound the PLO to no quasi-state building political activity and no direct challenges against Jordanian sovereignty. The PLO leadership was bound to keep order, but this assumed PLO control of its own elements. Naturally, even when it could exercise some control, the PLO's officials would look the other way since radical behavior on the part of smaller groups attracted recruits and funding. It stood to reason, therefore, that inevitably the agreement would be stillborn.

King Hussein then tried a broader diplomatic approach, traveling to the United States in April 1969 in order to explore the potential for a political solution to the West Bank occupation. This ultimately led to nothing.

The king followed that up with one or two further efforts to coordinate PLO military activity with the Jordanian armed forces, at least on a level of tactical liaison. He hoped at least to try and curb what was beginning to look a little like organized crime, in terms of illegal taxation, turf wars and political enforcement, but again, it all came to nothing. The PLO simply lacked sufficient internal discipline and centralized control to put any agreements reached into widespread effect.

From Arafat's point of view, he was duty bound to maintain a belligerent and uncompromising position toward Israel, and any perception that he was drifting toward a moderate stance, such as placing curbs on PLO activity in respect of King Hussein's concerns regarding Israeli reprisals, would simply undermine his own position. Thus, he adopted an approach of saying much and doing little, and all the while, King Hussein remained unable to fundamentally control this large, independent, and growing armed presence in his territory.

February 1970 saw the commencement of regular and heavy armed clashes between Jordanian police and Palestinian groups. A warning was issued to the Palestinians by the Jordanian government, but the king's authority was consistently undermined by the growing and vocal support of other Arab leaders and states for the Palestinian militants. King Hussein then felt compelled to approach the Israelis, finding, ironically, that his friends were more hostile than his enemies. The question was put to the Israelis through the American Embassy in Tel Aviv what their reaction would be if King Hussein ordered his army to move against the PLO. His fear was obviously that if he launched a civil war against Palestinian militants in his country, the Israelis would seize the opportunity to attack him. Seeing some strategic advantage in the Jordanian army neutralizing their mutual enemy on his own territory, the Israelis opted not to take advantage of a situation whereby King Hussein withdrew his loyal forces from the border in order to direct them elsewhere.

It must be remembered that the Jordanian armed forces, at a rank and file level, was made up largely of Palestinians, and it was only the British trained Bedouin units that the King was able to trust entirely. Thus, it was a very risky maneuver for King Hussein to contemplate an armed solution to this crisis, and it is a measure of how dangerous the situation had become, and how desperate he had become.

At the same time, the Israelis offered no commitment to limit their cross-border reprisal attacks, which continued. An exchange of Israeli and Jordanian artillery in early June 1970 threatened to escalate, and that would not have served the beleaguered king. He reined in his forces and again approached the Israelis through the American Embassy. His message was simply that he was doing all that he could to contain PLO activities in Jordan, and that direct Israeli aggression, even if it were in response to PLO attacks, did absolutely nothing to help. Could the Israelis not see their way clear to avoid complicating an already complicated situation? The American put pressure on the Israelis to comply, and they agreed to do so.

By then, clashes between various Fedayeen, and Jordanian troops and police had become a daily occurrence. On June 9, 1970, against a backdrop of increasing tension, and growing Palestinian confidence, the Fedayeen attacked the headquarters of the Jordanian General Intelligence Directorate, the Mukhabarat. The next day, as King Hussein drove to visit the site, his motorcade came under attack by the Fedayeen, resulting in the death of one of his bodyguards, although he himself escaped unhurt.

Clearly, matters were now coming quickly to a head. Loyal units shelled the two refugee camps of Al-Wehdat and Al-Hussein, which soon escalated into a full-scale action, lasting three days. Hundreds of deaths were recorded, in some reports up to 700, many of which were non-combatant Palestinian women and children. It was an ugly and potentially incendiary situation.

The Palestinians by then were fielding light artillery, mortars, and Katyusha rockets, and according to Israeli intelligence, typically very reliable in such matters, there were around 2,000 heavily Fedayeen in Amman alone, a veritable army. The PLO naturally made fertile use of the propaganda potential of all of this, and before long the Jordanian authorities were fielding accusations of provoking a massacre.

In due course, a ceasefire was agreed to and an armistice signed, which precipitated a brief lull in the fighting. The Popular Front for the Liberation of Palestine, however, would not comply, and its militants control of two hotels in downtown Amman, seizing a number of British, American and West German guests hostage. PFLP militants then threatened to blow up both buildings, demanding the dissolution of the Jordanian government and the disbanding of Jordanian special force units.

Members of the PFLP in 1969

Again, King Hussein found himself pressured from all sides. Arafat, who had begun to field criticism himself for being too willing to negotiate and concede, openly took the side of the PFLP. King Hussein then attempted to compromise, walking a very thin line between appeasing his Arab allies and keeping control of his country. He agreed to a dissolution of the government, and as the hostages walked free, he appointed a moderate, pro-Palestinian army general as chief-of-staff, and a Palestinian Prime Minister, Abdelmunim Al-Rifai, who in turn included six Palestinians in his cabinet.

This was a very risky move, not least because it set a precedent, but King Hussein was backed into a corner, and without friends, he had little choice. Observing it all from across the Atlantic, the Americans, ostensibly allied to Jordan, began to shake their heads, already starting to regard King Hussein as a dead man walking. The Fedayeen would obviously not stop at this. With one major concession in the bag, it was just a matter of time. Western powers began to consider the nature of a post-Hussein, Soviet-aligned Jordan in the wider Middle East equations. So, for that matter, did the Israelis. Even members of the king's own family began to see the downfall of the Hashemites in Jordan as inevitable.

However, King Hussein, to the surprise of many, handled the crisis with a degree of diplomatic dexterity that few thought capable. On July 10, another ceasefire accord was negotiated and signed between him and Arafat that appeared to push the Palestinian envelope yet further. It legitimized the presence of the PLO in Jordan in exchange for the establishment of a committee that would monitor and control Fedayeen activities in Jordan. This, under the circumstances, was of very limited value, but King Hussein was carefully guiding the situation toward a denouement.

The weeks passed, and a complicated diplomatic exchange between the Egyptians, the Americans, the Jordanians and the various PLO elements played out. It all seemed to have about it the air of a pantomime, with each party speaking a rehearsed set of lines to a prearranged script. A ceasefire was agreed between Egypt and Israel, as the ostensible end of the Six-Day War, and the War of Attrition that followed, but again this seemed more hot air than realpolitik. Arafat, in disgust at the apparent capitulation of Egypt's General Nasser (only apparent, for Nasser remained committed to war), uttered his now infamous comment: 'We have decided to convert Jordan into a cemetery for all conspirators – Amman shall be the Hanoi of the revolution.'

August closed with another major clash between Palestinian and Jordanian forces, with a Fedayeen ambush of an army convoy and an armed attack staged against the main post office in Amman.

September 1970 opened with another assassination attempt against King Hussein, the second such attempt in just three months. The attack took place in the town of Sweileh, northeast of Amman. The king was unhurt, although a driver was injured, and Hussein is said to have leapt out of the car and fired back at his attackers. This, however, simply prompted a renewed round of bitter clashes militants and Jordanian forces that continued until September 6.

Then, on the morning of September 6, 1970, fighting briefly ceased as both sides paused, and their jaws dropped. That morning, the world woke to extraordinary news of the hijacking of three international airliners by Palestinian militants. Members of the Popular Front for the Liberation of Palestine had taken control of TWA Flight 741 from Frankfurt to New York and Swissair Flight 100 from Zurich to New York. Both flights were diverted to a disused British military airfield, Dawson Field, located about-20 miles northeast of Amman in the Jordanian desert.

The audacity of these operations was astonishing. A little later, Pan Am Flight 93 from Amsterdam to New York was hijacked, also by members of the PFLP, and diverted first to Beirut, and then to Cairo. At more or less the same time, officials and crew of the Israeli national carrier, El Al, foiled a fourth hijacking attempt on an aircraft flying from Amsterdam. Three days later, on September 9, a PFLP sympathizer, in a hijacking not necessarily coordinated with the others, seized a British Overseas Airways Corporation flight in Bahrain and directed it to Dawson's field.

Jordan was suddenly at the center of world attention. The hijackers renamed Dawson Field Revolution Airport, and the following day, on September 7, they held a press conference for the large numbers of international press that had assembled during the course of the previous 24 hours. Prior to that, Jewish, American, Israeli, West German and Swiss passengers were separated out, with the remainder released. Jewish, non-Israeli passport holders were asked their religion. Most were from New York, and most answered truthfully. All Jews were held separately.

A spokesman for the hijackers claimed that the objective of the hijacking was to secure the release of political prisoners held in Israeli, U.S., Swiss, British and West German jails. The surviving hijacker of the El Al flight, a woman by the name of Layla Khalid, a well-known Palestinian militant, was detained in Britain when the flight landed at Heathrow, and her release was likewise demanded. A call was also made for the overthrow of King Hussein and the Hashemite Dynasty of Jordan.

According to some accounts, it was also communicated to the outside world that American hostages would only be released upon Israel's full compliance with the demands. Since Israel, and the United States, had a standing policy of no negotiation, the United States responded by placing a rapid response unit on high alert, ordering the Sixth Fleet into the Mediterranean and sending warplanes to Turkey.

The British, under the leadership of Prime Minister Edward Heath, something of a dove in international relations, opted to negotiate. It was agreed that Layla Khaled and others would be released in exchange for British hostages, which infuriated both the Israelis and the Nixon administration, and it pitched the Anglo-American relationship to a historic low.

30 miles away, in the meanwhile, in downtown Amman, PFLP militants seized control of the Intercontinental Hotel, snatching 125 hostages. A few days later, on September 10, fierce fighting between militants and Jordanian security erupted in and around the hotel grounds.

With terrorist holding hostages in the capital, and aircraft hijacked, and held at an abandoned airfield outside the capital, Jordan appeared to be on the very brink of a civil war. The United Nations, in the meanwhile, reacted with a bout of desperate handwringing that resulted in the hasty adoption without a vote of Resolution 286, vaguely calling for the release of all hostages in Jordan, without exception.

On September 12, the hijackers removed all 371 hostages from the aircraft and released all but 54, who were held for a further two weeks in nearby PFLP camps. The empty aircraft were then blown up in front of the press.

To all of this, there were mixed reactions in the Arab world. Most Arab governments, and Arafat on behalf of the PLO, privately disapproved of the hijackings, feeling that they had caused more harm than good to Palestinian cause, although Arafat rather unenthusiastically endorsed them publicly, mindful of public opinion. Official Arab condemnation was muted.

By then, however, King Hussein was approaching a point of decision. One way or another, the growing threat of armed Palestinian groups in Jordan had to be addressed. From numerous assassination attempts, to the hijacking of international airliners and the seizure of hostages in city hotels, the matter had clearly come to a head. There was also now a window of opportunity for him to justify action against the PLO in Jordan. In general, the hijackings had not been well received internationally, and if there was a moment to act, that moment was now.

On September 15, he convened an emergency meeting of his cabinet and military chiefs, and after lengthy discussions, he received the go-ahead to issue the order. It was estimated by the army that an operation to clear the Fedayeen out of the major Jordanian cities would take three days, and no more.

From there, King Hussein moved quickly. He dissolved the government and introduced military rule. He then invited the Fedayeen to disarm and leave the capital, which they refused to do, at which point he declared martial law throughout the country. On the morning of September 17, 1970, loyal Jordanian units were given the green light to move in.

Having made the decision to act, King Hussein acted definitively. Tanks of the Jordanian 60th Armoured Brigade entered the capital and approached the two refugee camps of Al-Wehdat and Al-Hussein from different directions. The two Palestinian strongholds were then pounded fairly indiscriminately by a combination of tanks, mortars, and artillery, supported by periodic airstrikes. It was a heavy and decisive bombardment that took the Palestinians by surprise. The Fedayeen were numerically strong, and well-armed with small arms, but they were uncoordinated, and they lacked any answer to the heavy armor, air assets and artillery that they were now facing. Fighting in and around Amman lasted for 10 days, and Jordanian forces simultaneously launched attacks against other Fedayeen controlled cities elsewhere in the country, including Irbid and Jerash in the north, As-Salt, and Zarqa, to the northwest and northeast of Amman respectively. Tanks proved to be of limited use in tight urban conditions of the capital and surrounding cities, and as the conventional attacks against the refugee camps continued, fighting elsewhere devolved into bitter street fighting as the various Fedayeen formed units and spread out.

In the camps, the Fedayeen were armed with a variety of mortars, Katyusha rockets, and outdated missiles that were fired sporadically into central Amman and surrounding cities. The fighting was brutal, sustained, and bloody, but within a few days, there were signs that the Fedayeen were beginning to fall back and disperse, with many crossings into Lebanon and Syria, and others crossing into the West Bank to surrender to the Israelis.

Meanwhile, there were a few interesting anomalies associated with this frenetic and violent 10 days. Obviously, the three-day timeframe predicted by army chiefs fell apart almost immediately. The Jordanians, however, sensed, at last, an opportunity to clear the PLO out of the country altogether, while the factions within the PLO sensed an opportunity to finish the fight that had been ongoing for several years and oust the Hashemite government of the country and replace it with a revolutionary administration. Both sides, therefore, fought bitterly.

The states neighboring Jordan obviously showed a keen interest in the progress of the war. The Israelis, the Syrians, and the Iraqis were each aware of their own strategic interests and for an opportunity for territorial gain. An Iraqi expeditionary force of some 100 tanks and 17,000 men was deployed in the country, near the town of Al-Mafraq, but it did not engage. The Iraqi position was generally pro-Palestinian, and their presence on Jordanian soil was a source of considerable concern.

Also in the country was a Pakistani training mission, headed by Brigadier Muhammad Zia-ul-Haq, who would later rule Pakistan from 1978-1988. From 1969-1970, he was stationed in Jordan assisting in training Jordanian tank units. He also commanded the Jordanian 2nd Division and played a minor, but notable role in the war, both in an advisory and planning capacity.

The role of Brigadier Zia-ul-Haq in the Black September crisis has been the subject of enormous controversy. The official Pakistani military position is this role was strictly in planning and fire allocation capacities, while Palestinian militant and Pakistani opposition propaganda state that he left Jordan soon after the war, his hands dripping with the blood of Palestinian children. In fact, Brigadier Zia-ul-Haq lent a hand when asked, and certainly did not extend his involvement much beyond observer and advisor in a situation where King Hussein needed all the help he could get.

More interesting, perhaps, was the role played by the Syrians. By June of 1970, the United States had already begun to put in place plans to intervene in Jordan on behalf of King Hussein if Syria or Iraq were to actively intervene or launch an opportunist attack at any point in the unfolding crisis. The Iraqis were there ostensibly as part of an informal military cooperation, but obviously, there was a wider strategic logic to their presence too. In the regional power equation, Jordan was rather the poor relation, insofar as her tank inventory, for example, comprised no more than 300 British Centurion and U.S. M-60 tanks, against a much more robust and modern Syrian and Iraqi Soviet-supplied arsenal. The Jordanian air force also weighed poorly against both the Syrian and Iraqi air forces, and so, under the circumstances, Jordan was extremely vulnerable.

As the first, crucial days of the way played out, a parallel war of rhetoric between Iraq and Syria on one side, and Jordan on the other began to give substance to fears of an imminent invasion by one or both of these neighboring countries. President Hashim al-Atasi of Syria announced that his country would 'spare no blood' to aid the Palestinians, and on September 17, as the fighting commenced, Radio Damascus reported that the Syrian foreign ministry had warned Jordan's ambassador that the 'Syrian revolution cannot remain silent or idle about the massacres to which the Palestine revolution groups and the masses in Jordan are being exposed.'

This certainly was fighting talk, and behind it lay an obvious Syrian interest in a quick Palestinian victory. This, again, had mostly to do with the ambiguous position that Jordan occupied in the Middle East, mainly in regards to the generally pro-western position of King Hussein, and the general distrust this provoked among Jordan's leftist, Ba'athist revolutionary neighbors. None of it, of course, was helped by Jordan's tendency to run hot and cold over the question of Israel, which would be revealed perhaps more acutely during Black September than at any other time. There was also the question of Syrian and Iraqi interests in Jordanian territory, and the fact that a Palestinian Jordan would finally settle the vexed question of a Palestinian state.

All of these issues alternated in importance at this critical juncture in September 1970. Jordanian armed forces, in the meanwhile, while making slow progress, were nonetheless succeeding in dislodging the various Fedayeen from their bases and from the major cities. The situation, however, remained critical, and one can suppose that the Syrians felt that a short campaign in support of the Palestinians would tip the balance in favor of the Palestinians, and secure that quick victory.

On September 20, during the fiercest fighting, a reinforced division of Syrian tanks began to move toward the Jordanian frontier, entering Jordanian territory at 2:00 a.m. Some 170 Syrian Soviet T-55 Tanks and 16,000 troops supported the invasion, although, surprisingly, the Syrians stopped short of committing their air force, even after Jordanian aircraft began running sorties against them.

The Syrian invasion, however, seemed to be tentative and uncommitted, and although there must have been some liaison between the two, the Iraqi expeditionary force already in Jordan remained uncommitted. In fact, the entire Iraqi force shifted eastwards, closer to the Iraqi border, in order to remain unequivocally out of the fight. It was also reported that, as the Syrian 6th Armored Brigade began moving toward Al-Mafraq, located just a few miles from the Syrian Border, Iraqi officers asked Jordanian air force units stationed at a nearby airfield to operate from another forward airbase in order that Iraqi forces in the vicinity not be drawn into the contest.

As any observer of Middle Eastern security matters would agree, this represented Arab regional diplomacy in its quintessential form, and the Syrians no doubt felt acutely isolated in the absence of Iraqi commitment. Why the Iraqis did not commit remains unclear.

As all of this was taking place, King Hussein launched an immediate appeal through various diplomatic channels, even Israeli channels, for outside military assistance. This, of course, put Israel in an interesting position, but in the order of things, a Hashemite ruled Jordan was a better prospect than a Palestinian or Ba'athist ruled Jordan, so the Israelis declared themselves open to suggestion. The suggestion simply was that a massing of Israeli troops on the Syrian border and demonstrative Israeli Air Force overflights close to the Syrian border would provide enough incentive for the Syrians to beat a hasty retreat in order to support their own security.

According to the later recollections of Henry Kissinger, who at the time was President Nixon's National Security Advisor, the Americans lacked the intelligence or targeting information to launch a support operation itself. This might well have been true, but one can also assume that Kissinger had one eye on the Soviets and the other on the Israelis, and he no doubt hoped that threat and bluff would be enough to educate the Syrians on the error of their ways.

By September 21, however, the second day of the Syrian invasion, the Syrians were somewhat better positioned. They now had some 300 tanks and 60 artillery pieces concentrated in northern

Jordan, near the towns of Irbid and Ramtha, although they seemed to be under orders neither to advance nor engage and apart from sporadic air operations, they were uninvolved in any of the consequential fighting. By the 21st, also, the movement of American naval and air assets into the eastern Mediterranean had become difficult not to observe. The Syrians were demanding the removal of the Sixth Fleet from the region, which must have caused Kissinger to chuckle to himself as the news of it came through.

As the battle for Jordan raged on, King Hussein continued to plead for U.S. or British air support against the Syrian advance. Kissinger was wary, unable to entirely interpret a complete lack of response from Moscow to the crisis, and this he tended to believe was evidence of a conspiracy. The Soviets, however, were wary of direct intervention, sensing also the possibility that the Israelis were awaiting an opportunity to advance into Jordan in order to seize more territory. While anxious for help from any quarter, King Hussein also understood that Israeli involvement would come with a price tag, but that was a risk he was prepared at that point to run. Israeli Prime Minister Golda Meir agreed to an Israeli intervention on condition that if the Soviets or the Egyptians took advantage of Israeli distraction to attack, the United States would directly intervene.

Thus, the Israelis went ahead and assembled an operational group comprising 200 tanks, which the Syrian quite naturally observed, as they did Israeli flyovers that menaced their tank units inside Jordanian territory. At the same time, a lack of consensus in Damascus (Syrian defense minister Hafez al-Assad did not support the intervention and refused to order air support) continued to undermine the effectiveness of the Syrian deployment.

The U.S., for its part, continued offering only diplomatic support to Israel and promised to veto any condemnation in the United Nations Security Council should Israel directly intervene. And while no specific promises were made, it was also pointed out to Israel that the U.S. Sixth Fleet, with various augmentations, lay off the coast of Lebanon. U.S. diplomatic language in the matter ran along these lines: "We have and will continue to make clear to the Soviets our support for Israel's security and integrity and its right to live within defensible borders. In the present crisis, the U.S. has augmented the Sixth Fleet; it has also taken other readiness measures. These clearly imply a decision not to permit Soviet intervention in the conditions under discussion. As for specific measures the U.S. may take to prevent Soviet intervention, these would depend on the circumstances and the situation that exists at the time. We have contingency plans for these eventualities."

In the end, no one intervened on the Jordanian side, and Jordanian forces, utilizing air and armor, successfully contained and halted the Syrian invasion in what can only be seen as a heroic and desperate defense. The Jordanian tank and aircraft inventory were rather archaic and certainly limited in numbers, and had the Syrians given their all, it is unlikely that they could have been stopped. By then, however, Jordanian airstrikes (some 250 sorties were flown during the crisis) were beginning to tell, and Israeli reconnaissance flights were reporting that logistical and resupply difficulties were also beginning to impact the Syrian armored columns. This, of course, also tends to imply a sluggish commitment and ongoing disagreement in Damascus.

On the evening of September 22, Syrian tank columns began crossing back into Syrian territory, and the situation changed almost overnight. Although King Hussein still requested air support, Israeli intervention suddenly seemed a great deal less desirable, and if the Israelis had harbored ambitions beyond simply intimidating the Syrians, the moment had passed.

In the aftermath of the war, historians and analysts have pointed to a combination of factors that caused the Syrian withdrawal. The U.S. naval surge certainly was a factor, as were the unexpected ferocity of Jordanian resistance and perhaps mixed messages emanating from Moscow. According to a memorandum forwarded by Kissinger to Nixon, King Hussein offered his thanks to the Israelis and the Americans for what he described as a successful "spooking" operation that he suggested contributed most to the Syrian withdrawal. He also requested that the United States express Jordanian gratitude to Israel while advising that he no longer required Israeli assistance.

The Fedayeen suffered heavy casualties, and many key commanders were either captured or killed. Interestingly, some 300 Jordanian troops defected to the Fedayeen, which was a small number given the large numbers of Palestinians serving in the Jordanian armed forces.

Within a week or so, the Arab states collected their wits began to respond. Almost entirely, the Arab community came out in support of the Palestinians, and King Hussein began to suffer increasing censure for his perceived massacre of Palestinians. It became clear to him then that the substantive military phase of the operation was over. An emergency Arab League summit was convened on September 27, during which King Hussein and Arafat signed a ceasefire agreement brokered by President Nasser. The agreement did not specify detailed terms, which would be negotiated later. Both sides were anxious to halt the fighting.

Two further matters of interest occurred at or around this summit. King Hussein, who personally attended the summit only after his Prime Minister, Muhammad Daoud, defected to Libya the day before the convening of the summit, was met with almost universal hostility from the Arab leaders who attended. The summit was even boycotted by Iraq, Syria, Algeria, and Morocco. Secondly, Egyptian President Gamal Nasser died within hours of the signing from a heart attack. His death would make way for the ascension of his deputy Anwar Sadat to the office of Egyptian President. Sadat would introduce a new era in the Middle East as he sought to redirect Egypt from the Soviet to the American sphere of influence.

As operations wound down, Arafat and the PLO emerged in a stronger position in regards to international sympathy and support, in particular among Arab nations, not one of which voiced open support for Jordan. Nonetheless, Palestinian aspirations to gain control of the country were gone, and in a second agreement, called the Amman Agreement, signed on October 13, Palestinian liberties in Jordan were severely limited. This was the preamble to the permanent expulsion of the PLO from Jordan.

King Hussein, militarily and politically, emerged the clear winner, and while his standing in the Arab world was in no way enhanced, his leadership thereafter faced less of a challenge, and his skill and judgment in steering his nation successfully through the crisis were tacitly acknowledged. Western powers had not offered him much hope of surviving, so when he did, he was more highly regarded.

Under the terms of the agreement, the Fedayeen undertook to respect Jordanian sovereignty and the king's authority, to withdraw their forces from towns and villages, to not wear identifying insignia or uniforms, and to refrain from bearing arms in public or outside their camps. In return, Jordan agreed to recognize the PLO as the sole, legitimate representative of the Palestinian people and to grant amnesty to the Fedayeen for incidents that had occurred during the civil war.

The Aftermath

"Black September was not a terrorist organization, but was rather an auxiliary unit of the resistance movement, at a time when the latter was unable to fully realize its military and political potential. The members of the organization always denied any ties between their organization and Fatah or the PLO." – Salah Khalaf, Stateless.

The civil war caused enormous material damage to Jordan, and the number of deaths and casualties, although fiercely disputed, was certainly high. Arafat claimed that as many as 25,000 Palestinians lost their lives, but most accounts agree that the Palestinian death toll was between 2,500 and 3,500, with Jordanian military deaths at 537.

Even still, the Amman Agreement was not the end of it. George Habash of the Popular Front for the Liberation of Palestine (PFLP) and Nayef Hawatmeh of the Democratic Front for the Liberation of Palestine (DFLP) did not acknowledge the agreement, and clashes between these two organizations and the Jordanian army continued, particularly in Amman, Irbid, and Jarash, where guerrilla forces had their main bases.

Operations between the Jordanian armed forces continued through the remainder of 1970 and into the first half of 1971, as the army continued in its efforts to drive the Fedayeen out of populated areas. The militants, however, were, for all intents and purposes, on the run, and by April 1971, King Hussein was reasonably confident in announcing that all Palestinian militants had been cleared out of Amman.

Sensing ultimate defeat, Fatah issued a statement calling for the overthrow of what it described as "the puppet separatist authority" of Jordan, calling for "national rule" in Jordan. Prime Minister Tal then effectively threw out the Cairo and Amman agreements, and under orders from King Hussein, he went for the Fedayeen's jugular, attacking the last substantive bases located in the Ajlun region, about 30 miles northwest of Amman. On July 19, 1971, the government announced that the remainder of the bases in northern Jordan had been destroyed and that 2,300 of the 2,500 Fedayeen had been arrested.

By then, most active Fedayeen had already left Jordan, some crossing the Jordan River and surrendering to the Israelis, but most shifting their bases and operations into southern Lebanon.

On November 28, 1971, the now infamous Black September organization, a splinter group of mainly Fatah fighters that took its name from the war of September 1970, assassinated Jordanian Prime Minister Wasfi Al-Tal. He was gunned down in the lobby of the Sheraton Hotel in Cairo while attending an Arab League summit. Black September had announced its existence, and more operations would follow, most notably at the Olympics in Munich in 1972.

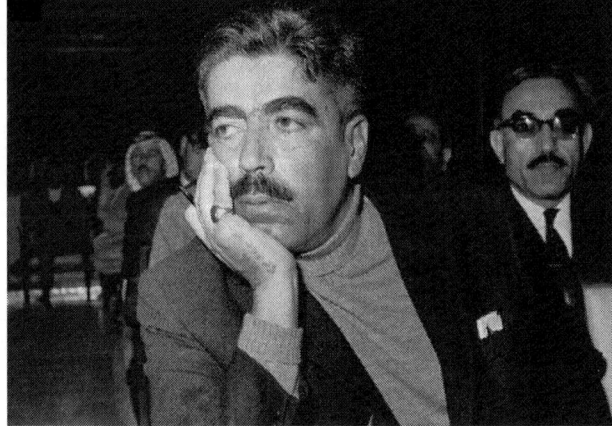

Prime Minister Tal

The removal of the PLO and all its associated factions from Jordan was the first major leadership challenge that King Hussein would face, and his survival finally established him as a presence in the Middle East, if not a particularly popular one. The enlarged PLO presence in southern Lebanon, however, critically destabilized that region, and it precipitated the Lebanese Civil War that would rage from 1975-1990. Fighting naturally intensified between Palestinians and Israelis along the Lebanese-Israeli border, while the PLO presence in Lebanon added a significant number of Muslims to a population traditionally multi-sectarian, one that had been reasonably balanced between Sunni and Shia Muslims, Christian and Druze.

The Lebanese leadership had tended to be dominated by a Maronite Christian elite, favored by a parliamentary structure established by the French during the Mandate period. The establishment of Israel, and the 1948 and 1967 exodus of Palestinian refugees from Israel to Lebanon, added strength to a Muslim political movement increasingly antagonistic toward Christian rule. The emergence of the Cold War added to tensions as the Christian Maronites tended to side with the West while leftist, pan-Arab Muslim groups moved increasingly toward the Soviet Union.

Fighting began in 1975 between Maronite and Palestinian forces, mainly of the PLO, who formed an alliance with those leftist, pan-Arabist and Muslim Lebanese groups. International powers such as Israel and Syria added their influence, as did various multinational and peacekeeping forces. The spark that ignited the powder keg, however, was the relocation and regrouping of Palestinian militant forces from Jordan, creating the very state of affairs in Lebanon that King Hussein of Jordan so feared in his country.

By then, the Black September organization had emerged as one of the most militant Palestinian terrorist organizations. Its signature operation was the Munich Massacre of 1972, during which, in a daring attack, 8 Black September terrorists seized and killed 11 Israeli athletes at the 1972 Munich Olympic Games. The operation reached a bloody climax on the evening of September 6 after a bungled German rescue operation. All surviving hostages were gunned down or blown up with hand grenades in two helicopters as the group was attempting to remove them from the country to Cairo for a handover of Palestinian political prisoners.

Black September was a shadowy and loosely configured organization, the nature and structure of which has been disputed by historians and journalists since it first appeared in 1972. It is generally regarded as a splinter group of Fatah, although some sources claim that it was simply a smokescreen used by Fatah to avoid direct complicity in certain operations. Other sources claim that it represented an ideological and tactical break from the traditional Fedayeen, with a more international complexion to its organization and structure.

Either way, it was an extremist group shut down by the PLO in September 1973, on the anniversary of its creation, ostensibly because of a withdrawal of the PLO from terrorist operations abroad.

Arafat would remain at the head of the Palestine Liberation Organization until his death in November 2004. King Hussein, having survived numerous assassination attempts, retained authority in Jordan until his death on February 7, 1999. The Hashemite Dynasty of Jordan survives under the rule of his son Abdulla II of Jordan, who, by his own account, is the 41st-generation direct descendant of the Prophet Muhammad.

Online Resources

Other Middle Eastern history titles by Charles River Editors

Other titles about the Yom Kippur War on Amazon

Further Reading
el Badri, Hassan (1979). The Ramadan War, 1973. Fairfax, Va: T. N. Dupuy Associates Books. ISBN 0-88244-600-2.
Bregman, Ahron (2002). Israel's Wars: A History Since 1947. London: Routledge. ISBN 0-415-28716-2.
Brook, Itzhak (2011). In the Sands of Sinai: a Physician's Account of the Yom Kippur War. Charleston: CreateSpace. ISBN 1-4663-8544-8.
Dupuy, Trevor Nevitt (1978). Elusive victory: The Arab–Israeli Wars, 1947–1974. San Francisco: Harper & Row. ISBN 0-06-011112-7.
Gawrych, George (2000). The Albatross of Decisive Victory: War and Policy Between Egypt and Israel in the 1967 and 1973 Arab-Israeli Wars. Greenwood Publishing Group. ISBN 0-313-31302-4.
Gawrych, Dr. George W. (1996). The 1973 Arab-Israeli War: The Albatross of Decisive Victory. Combat Studies Institute, U.S. Army Command and General Staff College.
Haber, Eitan; Schiff, Ze'ev (2003). Yom Kippur War Lexicon (in Hebrew). Or-Yehuda, Israel: Zmora-Bitan-Dvir. ISBN 978-965-517-124-2.
Hammad, Gamal (2002). al-Maʻārik al-ḥarbīyah ʻalá al-jabhah al-Miṣrīyah: (Ḥarb Uktūbar 1973, al-ʻĀshir min Ramaḍān) [Military Battles on the Egyptian Front] (in Arabic) (First ed.). Dār al-Shurūq.
Heikal, Mohamed (1975). The Road to Ramadan. London: Collins. ISBN 0-8129-0567-9.
Herzog, Chaim (2003) [1975]. The War of Atonement: The Inside Story of the Yom Kippur War. London: Greenhill Books. ISBN 978-1-85367-569-0.
Herzog, Chaim (1982). the Arab-Israeli Wars. Random House. ISBN 978-0-394-50379-0.
Herzog, Chaim (1989). Heroes of Israel. Boston: Little, Brown. ISBN 0-316-35901-7.
Insight Team of the London Sunday Times (1974). The Yom Kippur War. Garden City: Doubleday. ISBN 978-0-385-06738-6.
Israeli, Raphael (1985). Man of Defiance: A Political Biography of Anwar Sadat. London: Weidenfeld & Nicolson. ISBN 0-389-20579-6.
Israelyan, Victor (2003) [1995]. Inside the Kremlin During the Yom Kippur War. University Park, PA: Pennsylvania State University Press. ISBN 0-271-01737-6.
Karsh, Efraim (2002). The Iran-Iraq War, 1980–1988. Oxford: Osprey Publishing. ISBN 1-84176-371-3.
Lanir, Zvi (2002) [1983]. ha-Hafta'ah ha-basisit: modi'in ba-mashber [Fundamental Surprise: Intelligence in Crisis] (in Hebrew). Tel-Aviv: Hakibbutz Hameuchad. OCLC 65842089.
Morris, Benny (2001). Righteous Victims. New York: Vintage Books. ISBN 978-0-679-74475-7.
Ma'Oz, Moshe (1995). Syria and Israel: From War to Peacemaking. Oxford: Clarendon Press. ISBN 0-19-828018-1.
Neff, Donald (1988). Warriors against Israel. Brattleboro, Vermont: Amana Books. ISBN 978-0-915597-59-8.
Nicolle, David; Cooper, Tom (May 25, 2004). Arab MiG-19 and MiG-21 units in combat. Osprey Publishing. ISBN 1-84176-655-0.
Edgar O'Ballance. No Victor, No Vanquished: The Yom Kippur War (1979 ed.). Barrie & Jenkins Publishing. pp. 28–370. ISBN 978-0214206702.
Pape, Robert A (Fall 1997). "Why Economic Sanctions Do Not Work". International Security. 22 (2): 90. JSTOR 2539368. OCLC 482431341. doi:10.2307/2539368.

Quandt, William (2005). Peace Process: American diplomacy and the Arab–Israeli conflict since 1967. Washington, DC: Brookings Institution / Univ. of California Press. ISBN 0-520-22374-8.

Quandt, William B (May 1976). "Soviet Policy in the October 1973 War" (PDF). Rand Corp. R-1864-ISA. Archived from the original (PDF) on October 2, 2012.

Rabinovich, Abraham (2005) [2004]. The Yom Kippur War: The Epic Encounter That Transformed the Middle East. New York, NY: Schocken Books. ISBN 0-8052-4176-0.

al Sadat, Muhammad Anwar (1978). In Search of Identity: An Autobiography. London: Collins. ISBN 0-00-216344-6.

Shazly, Lieutenant General Saad el (2003). The Crossing of the Suez, Revised Edition (Revised ed.). American Mideast Research. ISBN 0-9604562-2-8.

Shlaim, Avi (2001). The Iron Wall: Israel and the Arab World. W. W. Norton & Company. ISBN 0-393-32112-6.

Rodman, David (2013). "The Impact of American Arms Transfers to Israel during the 1973 Yom Kippur War" (PDF). Israel Journal of Foreign Affairs, VII:3.

Free Books by Charles River Editors
We have brand new titles available for free most days of the week. To see which of our titles are currently free, click on this link.

Discounted Books by Charles River Editors
We have titles at a discount price of just 99 cents everyday. To see which of our titles are currently 99 cents, click on this link.

Made in United States
Troutdale, OR
12/26/2023